Veiled Chameleons
or Yemen Chameleons

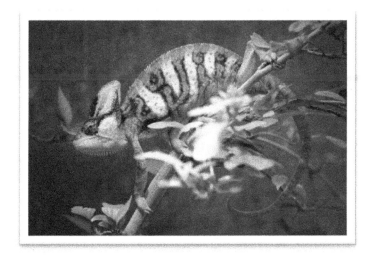

Facts and Information

The Complete Owner's Guide to the Veiled Chameleon or
Yemen Chameleon Including Keeping and Caring for as
Pets, Diet and Food, Breeding, Handling, Vivarium Setup,
Costs, Sizes and Much More.

Richard Pride

Copyright and Trademarks

Disclaimer and Legal Notice

Visit our website www.VeiledChameleonsCare.com for our contact details or if you are interested in becoming an affiliate for this book.

Acknowledgements

I would like to thank my wife and children for their endless love and support, especially my wife whose patience with me knows no bounds.

Foreword

Veiled chameleons are a species of chameleon native to Yemen, which is how they earned the nickname, Yemen chameleon. These chameleons are an attractive and colorful species known for their unique appearance and intriguing behaviors. If you have ever considered owning a non-traditional pet, the veiled chameleon is an excellent option. These reptiles are beautiful sight to behold and they can be incredibly rewarding as pets.

Whilst veiled chameleons make wonderful pets, they may not be the right choice for everyone. In this book you will learn the basics and veiled chameleon facts to help you determine whether this species is the right pet for you. Also included is a wealth of information about buying chameleons, creating a suitable habitat, feeding your pet and even breeding them. By the time you complete this book you will have a firm foundation of knowledge and understanding to help you get started in raising and caring for your very own veiled chameleon.

Table of Contents

Chapter One: Introduction

Also known as the Yemen chameleon, the veiled chameleon is a large species that is becoming increasingly popular as a pet. These lizards are bright green in color with splotches, spots and stripes of various colors all over the body. Where this species gets its nickname however is from the rigid veil that sits on top of the head. The official name for this species, Yemen chameleon, was given in reference to the chameleon's natural habitat in the mountainous regions of Yemen.

If you are looking for a unique and interesting pet, the veiled chameleon is definitely one to consider. Not only do these animals exhibit very different behaviors than traditional pets such as cats and dogs, they never fail to surprise. For example, the veiled chameleon is capable of changing color to blend with it's surroundings or as an indication of it's mood.

Veiled chameleons can be somewhat challenging to keep as pets, especially if you have never owned a reptile before. For this reason, it is important that you learn as much as you possibly can about these amazing creatures before you decide to bring one home.

Chapter Two: Understanding the Veiled Chameleon

Veiled chameleons require very specific care and cannot be handled in the same way as a more common pet such as a dog or cat. Even if you already have a good idea with regard to whether a veiled chameleon is right for you, you should give yourself, and your future chameleon, the courtesy of learning everything you can about them. This chapter includes veiled chameleon facts and information that you will find useful in understanding this beautiful species.

1) Facts about Veiled Chameleons

Yemen chameleons are so named because they can be found in the mountains of Yemen, though they also live in parts of Saudi Arabia and the United Arab Emirates. These reptiles carry the scientific name *Chamaeleo calyptratus*, which means they belong to the genus Chamaeleo within the Chamaeleonidae family. The family Chamaeleonidae contains over 150 different species of chameleon ranging in size and color. Even though these species are all very different in appearance, they share one common feature – their zygodactylous feet. This simply means their toes are arranged in such a way that the first and fourth face backward while the middle two face forward. This arrangement is also found in birds.

Like most chameleon species, the veiled chameleon is arboreal, which means they spend the majority of their life in trees. In fact the body of this species is specially adapted to this style of life. For example, the veiled chameleon's body is slightly flattened which, along with its green coloring, enables it to blend in with the leaves. The zygodactylous feet of this species are especially good for gripping the limbs and branches of trees as it climbs. Even the veiled chameleon's tail is useful in an arboreal habitat being prehensile, which means it can be used almost as a fifth appendage.

Two of the most identifiable features of the veiled chameleon, and of chameleons in general, are their swivel eyes and long tongue. The chameleon's eyes protrude from their head forming a round globe shape and are able to move independently of each other enabling the chameleon to see in front and behind itself at all times, therefore being able to keep an eye out for predators. Contrary to popular belief, chameleons do not have sticky tongues, they do however have a specialized muscle on the end of their tongue which enables them to catch insects. Veiled chameleons are ambush predators, meaning they lie in wait for prey to come by and then snatch it with their tongues.

These reptiles are technically omnivorous, though a standard veiled chameleon's diet consists largely of insects. Veiled chameleons will occasionally feed on fruit, leaves and blossom, though this usually occurs during times of drought or when water is scarce. You may find it interesting to know that veiled chameleons do not drink water in the same way that other animals do. Rather than drinking from puddles, pools or other bodies of water, veiled chameleons will only drink water droplets that form on leaves.

In comparison to other chameleon species, the veiled chameleon is very large. Males of the species can grow between 17 and 24 inches (43 to 61cm) long whilst females usually grow up to 10 to 14 inches (25 to 35.5cm). In terms of weight, male veiled chameleons are usually between 3.5 and 7 ounces (100 to 200g) whilst females are 3.2 to 4.2 ounces (90 to 120g). For both sexes, the tail accounts for a significant portion of the animal's total length. Both sexes also have a helmet-like growth on the head called a casque. The average life span of veiled chameleon is approx 5 years in captivity.

How Do Male and Female Veiled Chameleons Differ?

An interesting fact regarding veiled chameleons is they display a large degree of sexual dimorphism, meaning there are clear visible differences between the male and female sex of the same species. Whilst female Yemen chameleons are usually uniformly green in color, males are much more brightly colored. This uniform coloring also applies to baby and juvenile veiled chameleons. The only time a female is likely to exhibit bright coloring rivaling a male is during breeding. After a successful mating, and when the female is gravid (carrying eggs), she will change to dark green with yellow and blue spots all over the body.

If you see a blue veiled chameleon, it is almost certainly to be a male. Not only do the male of the species exhibit a brighter green coloring than females, they also have stripes, spots and splotches of blue, yellow and brown. Another feature that distinguishes the male from the female of the species, is the presence of a spur on the back of the heel on their hind feet. This spur is called a tarsal spur and is used during mating. In a baby male veiled chameleon, the spur is already present at birth and will grow as the chameleon matures.

Chapter Two: Understanding the Veiled Chameleon

a) Summary of Facts about Veiled Chameleons

- The scientific name for the veiled chameleon is *Chamaeleo calyptratus.*
- Also known as the Yemen chameleon, the veiled chameleon is one of over 150 chameleon species in its genus.
- Veiled chameleons are found primarily in the mountainous regions of Yemen, although can also live in Saudi Arabia and the United Arab Emirates.
- This species is omnivorous, although primarily feeds on insects.
- Unique physical attributes of this species include a helmet-like casque, zygodactylous feet, a prehensile tail, and swivel eyes.
- Males are both larger and more colorful than females.
- The average size for a male veiled chameleon is 17 to 24 inches (43 to 61 cm) and 3.5 to 7 ounces (100 to 200g).
- The average size for a female is 10 to 14 inches (25 to 35.5 cm) and 3.2 to 4.2 ounces (90 to 120g).
- Male veiled chameleons are bright green with patches or stripes of blue, yellow or brown color.

- Females of the species are dull green, exhibiting blue or yellow spots during breeding.
- The average veiled chameleon lifespan is about 5 years.

2) Veiled Chameleons in the Wild

The veiled chameleon is one of 80 species of chameleon referred to as Old World or "true" chameleons. The term "Old World" refers to species native to the parts of the world that were known to Europeans prior to the discovery of the Americas. The term "true" chameleon simply means that the species belong to the family Chamaeleonidae within the order Squamata – order is a taxonomic rank in the biological classification of species. This term is typically used to distinguish chameleons from anoles, small reptiles that also belong to the order Squamata.

The geographical range for veiled chameleons in the wild is between Yemen and Saudi Arabia, particularly along escarpments and in local wadis (river valleys). These chameleons are typically found in dry plateaus up to an elevation of 3,000 feet (914 m). Though veiled chameleons are arboreal, they can also be found living in bushes and shrubs close to the ground, they generally are inclined to live in some kind of foliage where they are protected from predators. One unique thing about the veiled chameleon is that it is adept to survive a much wider temperature range than other chameleons, between 75° and 95°F (24° to 35°C).

In the wild veiled chameleons are somewhat shy and when threatened, are likely to curl up into a ball. They may also darken in color as a warning sign to potential predators. Even after the threat has passed, it may take a long time for the chameleon to unfold and resume movement. In the presence of other chameleons however, veiled chameleons are not shy, they are very aggressive. The male of the species is incredibly territorial and prefers to live on it's own. The only occasion male and females of the species can be found close to each other is during Yemen chameleon breeding season.

a) Conservation Concerns for Chameleons

Though the veiled chameleon is not regarded as an endangered species (being listed as Least Concern on the IUCN Red List), there are some concerns regarding the long-term survival of the species in the wild. Growing human populations in the veiled chameleon's natural environment have resulted not only in destruction of their habitat, but also in increased competition for food and other resources. Though many native species are threatened by these changes, chameleons are particularly sensitive and do not find it easy adapting to change.

It is important to note that veiled chameleons, like all chameleons move very slowly. This being the case, it is difficult for them to relocate quickly if their habitat becomes affected. Chameleons tend to live in isolated pockets, not straying far from their homes, consequently habitat loss can be extremely devastating for native populations. Chameleons can also be exploited, by both local and foreign people, captured for sale in illegal pet trade or for use in rituals. There is also a growing demand by tourists for chameleon body parts.

3) Veiled Chameleon Origin and Evolution

The name "chameleon" is derived from the Latin *chamaeleo* - borrowed from various Greek words meaning "on the ground" and "lion". Modern chameleons belong to the family Chamaeleonidae which is divided into two sub-families, Brookesiinae and Chamaeleoninae. This division occurred in 1986 by Klaver and Bohme, but has since been the subject of much debate. Recently, authorities on the subject have rejected the division of the family Chamaeleonidae into sub-families.

Alhough a great deal regarding the evolution of the chameleon is unknown. The oldest chameleon fossil belonged to a now extinct species called *Anqingosaurus brevicephalus* which lived in China during the Middle Paleocene era (between 58.7 and 61.7 million years ago). Fossils dating back to the Lower Miocene period (between 13 and 23 million years ago) include *Chamaeleo caroliquarti* from Germany and the Czech Republic as well as *Chamaeleo intermedius* from Kenya during the Upper Miocene period (between 5 and 13 million years ago).

Fossils of chameleons place the oldest species between 58 and 61 million years ago, but scientists agree that these reptiles are most likely much older. It is commonly thought that modern chameleons shared an ancestor with agamids and iguanids over 100 million years ago. Although more than 50% of modern chameleon species can be found in Madagascar, chameleon fossils have been found throughout Africa, Europe and Asia. This suggests that chameleons were once more widespread than they are currently and that individual species may have evolved to adapt to their current environment after the dispersal.

a) Color Change in Chameleons

One of the most interesting adaptations that chameleons have evolved is the ability to change their color. Whilst it was long assumed that chameleons changed color as a means of camouflage, it is now known that these reptiles change color in response to a variety of stimulus. Not only do they change color in response to predators, but also as a result of changes in mood, temperature, and other environmental conditions. For example, chameleons tend to exhibit darker colors when they are angry or threatened and lighter colors during mating.

Fascinatingly, the process that produces the different colors of veiled chameleons, involves the use of specialized cells called chromatophores. These are located in three layers beneath the skin and contain various pigments. Cells in the upper layer are called xanthophores or erythrophores and contain yellow and red pigments, iridophores and guanophores, found in the second layer contain blue and white pigment and finally cells in the third layer, melaophores contain dark melanin pigments. The color change of the chameleon is determined by the distribution of the pigments in these cells.

4) Types of Pet Chameleons

Though the veiled chameleon is very popular, it is not the only type of chameleon commonly kept as a pet. Below you will find a list of other popular pet chameleons as well as basic information about each species:

Flap-Necked Chameleon

Panther Chameleon

Fischer's Chameleon

Carpet Chameleon

Meller's Chameleon

Jackson's Chameleon

Oustalet's Chameleon

Four-Horned Chameleon

Flap-Necked Chameleon

These are fairly small compared to the veiled chameleon, growing only as long as 13 inches (33 cm). They also have a shorter lifespan, between 2 and 3 years. This species is native to southern Africa and tend to thrive well in captivity.

Panther Chameleon

The panther chameleon is native to Madagascar where it is acclimatized to higher temperatures and humidity than the veiled chameleon. This species grows fairly large, up to 20 inches (50.8 cm) for males. The average lifespan for a panther chameleon is 5 to 7 years and they tend to adjust better around people than veiled chameleons.

Fischer's Chameleon

This species of is found in Tanzania and Kenya where they are accustomed to moderate temperatures and humidity. Fischer's chameleons grow up to 15 inches (38 cm) and live up to 3 years. This species is only recommended for experienced owners.

Carpet Chameleon

The carpet chameleon is also found in Madagascar and is very small compared to the veiled chameleon, growing only up to 9 inches (23 cm) in length. Carpet chameleons live only 2 to 3 years but they are very hardy and make good pets.

Meller's Chameleon

The Meller's chameleon is an east African species where they are used to warm temperatures. These chameleons are very large, growing up to 24 inches (61 cm) and have a lifespan of up to 12 years. This species is very aggressive.

Jackson's Chameleon

This chameleon is native to east Africa, although it has also been introduced to Hawaii. The Jackson's chameleon grows up to 13 inches (33 cm) and lives up to 8 years. This species is readily available and typically does well in captivity.

Oustalet's Chameleon

This species of chameleon is native to Madagascar and it is one of the largest, growing up to 30 inches (76 cm) long. Oustalet's chameleons live up to 12 years in captivity and normally make good pets if you have the space to accommodate them.

Four-Horned Chameleon

This species is native to Cameroon where they are accustomed to warm temperatures and relatively high humidity. The four-horned chameleon lives for about 5 years and grows up to 14 inches (35.5 cm) long. These chameleons are very attractive and often do well in captivity as long as its requirements are met.

a) Pros and Cons of Veiled Chameleon vs. Other Species

After reading about some of the other chameleon species commonly kept as pets, you may be wondering how the veiled chameleon compares. Below you will find a list of pros and cons for the veiled chameleon in comparison to other species.

Pros:

- Moderate lifespan, not a long-term commitment such as the Oustalet's Chameleon.
- Tends to fair well in captivity under the right circumstances.
- Highly attractive, more colorful than other chameleon species.
- Gender dimorphism makes it easier to identify males from females.

Cons:

- Grows larger than some chameleon species, requires a great deal of space.
- May not tolerate handling as well as the Panther Chameleon.
- Generally fairly aggressive and not recommended for inexperienced reptile owners.
- Very territorial, cannot be kept with other chameleons or other pet reptiles.

Chapter Three: Practical Information about Veiled Chameleons

Now that you know the basics regarding veiled chameleons as animals, you are ready to move on to some more practical information about this species as a pet. Before you decide whether or not this is the right species for you, you need to learn everything you can about caring for veiled chameleons. In this chapter you will receive information about licensing requirements for these animals, advice about veiled chameleon cost, frequently asked questions and the pros and cons for this species.

1) Licensing Requirements for Chameleons

The veiled chameleon is not your typical pet, so you may be wondering whether you need a special license or permit to keep one. In actual fact, this will depend on where you live. Certain areas may require a reptile keeper's license (or something similar), while others will not. The one thing you do not want is to bring your veiled chameleon home, only to have him confiscated because you have not followed the correct licensing procedure. In this section you will learn whether or not a license is required to keep veiled chameleons as pets in the U.S. and in the U.K. You will also receive advice for obtaining a license if one is necessary.

a) Licensing in the U.S.

There are no federally regulated licensing requirements for pets in the United States – everything is mandated at the state or local level. This being the case, you will need to check with your local council to ascertain if a license or permit to keep veiled chameleons as pets in your particular area is a requirement. However, you will likely find the U.S. generally does not require a permit to keep reptiles as pets unless they are considered dangerous, endangered or native species. If you want to keep a caiman or an alligator for example, you would require a special permit, as these animals are considered dangerous. You would also need a permit if you wanted to keep a reptile native to the state in which you live, but since veiled chameleons are not considered an endangered or dangerous species and are not native to the U.S., it is unlikely you will need a permit or license to keep one.

b) Licensing in the U.K.

Whilst the U.K. does require licensing for dogs, there are no regulations regarding the keeping of reptiles as pets. You are free to keep, breed and sell reptiles as pets in the U.K. without a license as long as the species are not endangered, dangerous or native. The only item of legislation you are likely to encounter in the U.K. is the Animal Welfare Act of 2006 which was passed in an effort to reduce the prevalence of animal cruelty. It requires owners to provide their pets with a suitable environment, a healthy diet and the ability to exhibit normal behaviors.

2) Frequently Asked Questions

Below you will find a list of frequently asked questions related to some of the more practical aspects of keeping veiled chameleons as pets. The answers to these questions may help you to determine whether this is the right pet for you.

Question: *How many veiled chameleons should I buy?*
Answer: As you have already learned, veiled chameleons can be fairly aggressive, especially the male of the species. In the wild, these chameleons live alone and the only time they come into contact with each other is during breeding season. This being the case, you should not plan to keep more than one veiled chameleon in the same vivarium. If however you do want to keep more than one, ensure you provide them with separate veiled chameleon cages and position them so they cannot see each other.

Question: *Can I keep multiple species of chameleon together?*
Answer: No - not only can you not keep more than one veiled chameleon together, but you should also avoid keeping your veiled chameleon with other species of chameleon. These reptiles can be very territorial and will not cope with sharing their territory with another

chameleon. Even if you provide your chameleons with a very large cage, the stress of having an "invader" in his territory could be very bad for your veiled chameleon.

Question: *Can my veiled chameleon be kept with other reptiles?*
Answer: You may be tempted to keep your veiled chameleon with other reptiles, but avoid this temptation. Smaller reptiles will either become prey or targets of aggression for your veiled chameleon, whilst larger reptiles could harm your pet. It is always best to keep a veiled chameleon in a cage entirely by itself.

Question: *Is it better to buy a male or female?*
Answer: There are several factors to consider in answering this question, but the primary issue is how much experience you have in caring for chameleons and how much extra effort you are willing to expend. Male chameleons may have issues with aggression but females may need extra care during the time when they are carrying eggs. Even without breeding, female veiled chameleons will lay eggs but will not be fertilized and will not hatch. Unless you are able to provide a suitable nesting box for your female chameleon, she will refuse to lay the eggs and will become egg bound – this is a very serious and deadly condition.

Question: *Are veiled chameleons good pets for children?*

Answer: The answer to this question largely depends on the age and maturity level of your child and on their expectations and requirements from a pet. If your child is expectant of a pet that will enjoy being handled and one which will play with him, a veiled chameleon is not the right choice. It is also important to consider that veiled chameleons require more care (of a more specialized kind) than cats or dogs, so it's worth considering whether or not your child can provide this. Finally, remember that veiled chameleons cannot be fully tamed, so there is always the risk of your child being bitten. Do not purchase a veiled chameleon for your child unless he is old enough to handle the responsibility and capable of implementing basic safety precautions and good hygiene practice.

Question: *Will I be able to handle my veiled chameleon?*

Answer: Yes you can handle your veiled chameleon but should take into account how often you do so, as you will need to consider the effect it may have on your pet. Veiled chameleons are not domestic pets so are unlikely to "enjoy" being handled. Depending on the temperament of your individual chameleon however, he may tolerate it. Regardless of how well your chameleon responds to handling, you should limit the frequency so as not to stress him.

3) Pros and Cons of Veiled Chameleons

No matter what type of pet you are considering, there will always be pros and cons to think about. Before you go out and buy a veiled chameleon, you will need to consider the good and not so good things about keeping one as a pet. Only when you are able to make an educated decision, should you make one at all. Below you will find general pros and cons of veiled chameleons as pets along with a comparison of male versus female:

Veiled Chameleon Pros

- Unique pets and very different from a "traditional" pets.
- Fascinating to observe, able to change colors, unique behaviors.
- Does not require additional space outside of an all-inclusive vivarium.
- Generally will not require a great deal of personal attention or interaction to limit handling.
- Lighting and heating can be automated using an automatic timer.
- Do not require any bathing or cleaning.

Veiled Chameleon Cons

- Must be housed in a cage by itself – no other chameleons or reptiles within sight.
- Fairly large and will require a cage big enough to accommodate its size.
- Specific requirements for cage conditions - lighting, temperature, humidity, etc.
- Will not drink water from bowls - cage must be misted daily.
- Not a good choice for inexperienced reptile owners and may not be an ideal pet for children.
- Can be very territorial and aggressive compared to other chameleon species.
- Eats mostly insects that you may need to buy in bulk or raise them yourself at home.

Pros/Cons for Male Veiled Chameleons

- More aggressive/territorial than females.
- Do not require specialized care in regard to egg-laying.
- Much larger than females and will require a larger cage.
- Cannot be kept with or near other chameleons.
- Much more colorful than females.

Pros/Cons for Female Veiled Chameleons

- Smaller than males by several inches, smaller cage.
- Requires specialized care during egg-laying periods, including a nesting box and adjusted diet.
- May tolerate other females or proximity to other chameleons (depending on personality).

4) Cost of Keeping Veiled Chameleons

One of the most important things you need to ask yourself before bringing a veiled chameleon home, is whether or not you can afford it. Not only do you have to cover the cost of your veiled chameleon, the cage, required supplies and regular cost of it's food, you will also need to consider the extra utilities costs to keep the cage running. In this section you will find information about the start-up costs to prepare for your veiled chameleon as well as the average monthly costs to provide for your pet.

a) Start-up Costs

The startup costs for a veiled chameleon will vary greatly depending on the quality of the items you choose. For example, you may be able to purchase a second-hand glass terrarium much cheaper than a mesh Yemen chameleon vivarium. In considering all your options however, you need to think about what is best for your pet's welfare. You may think that a little money can be saved in the beginning by cutting corners, but if your chameleon's environment is not ideal, then he will fail to thrive and may also fall ill which could lead to expensive vet bills. Below you will find a list of start-up costs for veiled chameleons as well as a table outlining the total cost.

Vivarium

As mentioned earlier, the cost for your veiled chameleon housing will depend on the size and the materials you choose. In Chapter Five you will learn more specifically about the size the vivarium will need to be, but make plans for one at least 2 x 2 x 4 feet (61 x 61 x 122 cm). Choosing a mesh reptile vivarium is far better, so you can expect to pay between $75 and $150 (£48.75 to £97.50) for one this size.

Enclosure Accessories

As you already know, veiled chameleons are arboreal creatures so spend most of their time in trees. For this reason, your veiled chameleon cage will require certain accessories to simulate the reptile's natural environment. Some accessories you may need to buy include living or artificial plants, branches or dowels, vines, basking rocks, etc. You will learn more about the specific plants for veiled chameleons in Chapter Five. Plan to spend between $50 and $100 (£32.50 to £65) on accessories for your veiled chameleon enclosure.

Veiled Chameleon Price

The purchase price of your veiled chameleon may vary greatly depending where you go. You are likely to pay more at a pet store than you would at a reptile trade show. If you are looking for a chameleon with certain colors or patterns, you may have to pay more to buy from a specialized breeder. For the most part however, you can expect to pay between $25 and $75 (£16.25 to £48.75) for your new pet.

Lighting/Heating

Aside from the enclosure itself, lighting and heating is perhaps the most important and significant start-up cost for your veiled chameleon. In order to keep your veiled chameleon healthy, you will need to maintain a certain temperature range and humidity within the enclosure, therefore, you will need to invest in a heating and lighting system. If you buy specialized reptile light fixtures at a pet store, you may find yourself paying twice as much as what you would if you bought the fixtures at your local home improvement store. This doesn't mean you are lowering the standard, it is simply a practical method of saving money. Where you should not try to save money is the cost of your UVB and heat lamp bulbs that are essential for your chameleon's health. To equip your veiled chameleon vivarium with adequate heating and lighting, you should expect to pay between $100 and $250 (£65 to £162.50).

Additional Equipment

Whilst heating and lighting is the most important equipment for your veiled chameleon enclosure, there are a few other essentials you may want to keep to hand. An automatic timer will save you from having to turn the lights on and off at certain times each day, a spray bottle to mist your chameleon's cage along with dishes for food if you plan to offer fruit or insects that will not move freely around the cage. The cost for these items will vary but you should budget $20 to $50 (£13 to £32.50) for additional equipment expenses.

Summary	Cost Range
Vivarium	$75 to $150 (£48.75 to £97.50)
Enclosure Accessories	$50 to $100 (£32.50 to £65)
Purchase Price	$25 to $75 (£16.25 to £48.75)
Lighting/Heating	$100 and $250 (£65 to £162.50)
Additional Equipment	$20 to $50 (£13 to £32.50)
Total Cost:	$270 to $625 (£176 to £406)

b) Monthly Costs

Though the startup costs for your veiled chameleon are the most significant, they are not the only costs you have to be concerned about, you will also have to pay for food, supplements, utilities associated with the vivarium and veterinary care for your chameleon on a regular basis. Below you will find an overview of the estimated monthly costs for keeping veiled chameleons as well as a table outlining the total estimated monthly cost.

<u>Food</u>

Unlike traditional pets, you cannot simply give your chameleon a bowl of dry food. A healthy Yemen chameleon diet consists of a wide variety of insects served alive. Your monthly food costs will vary depending on the type of insects you buy and how you buy them. Savings can be made, by buying in bulk and keeping and breeding the insects yourself at home. Adult veiled chameleons only eat 3 to 4 times per week, so you should budget a monthly food cost of approx $35 to $50 (£22.75 to £32.50).

<u>Supplements</u>

Whilst feeding your veiled chameleon a variety of insects will help to ensure he has a balanced diet, captive chameleons require supplements to round out their nutrition. These supplements come in powdered form and one container should last you at least a month, possibly longer. Therefore, you shouldn't have to spend more than $10 to $15 (£6.50 to £9.75) per month on supplements.

Utilities

Because the lights in your chameleon's enclosure will be on for 10 to 12 hours a day, you should expect your electricity bill to rise after bringing home your chameleon. The monthly cost for utilities associated with your chameleon's cage will vary depending on the rate you are paying per kWh and the wattage of the bulbs you use will generate. For the sake of budgeting, plan to pay anywhere between $0.25 to $1 (£0.38 to £0.65) per day for electricity, which averages between $8 and $30 (£5.20 to £19.50) per month.

Veterinary Care

As long as you provide your veiled chameleon with a suitable habitat, a healthy diet and adequate supplementation, he should not require regular veterinary care. If your chameleon does become sick however, you should expect to pay more for a visit to an exotics vet than you would for a normal vet. For the purpose of budgeting, plan for 1 visit to the vet per year at an average cost of $75 (£48.75) per examination – equating to approx $6.25 (£4) per month.

Other Costs

In addition to the cost of food, supplements, utilities, and veterinary care, there may be other expenses that occur occasionally. For example, one month you may need to repair a tear or crack in the screen of your vivarium. The next month you might have to buy extra plants to replace any that has died. These extra costs will vary each month but a budget of $15 (£9.75) per month should provide for any extra expenditure.

Summary	Cost Range
Food	$35 to $50 (£22.75 to £32.50)
Supplements	$10 to $15 (£6.50 to £9.75)
Utilities	$8 and $30 (£5.20 to £19.50)
Veterinary Care	$6.25 (£4)
Other Costs	$15 (£9.75)
Total Cost:	$74 to $116 (£48 to £76)

Chapter Four: Bringing Your Veiled Chameleon Home

After reading the last few chapters, you should now have a good understanding of what the veiled chameleon is and the requirements to keep them as pets. If you are confident that a veiled chameleon is right for you, in this chapter you will find helpful information in preparing for and buying your new pet, where to find Yemen chameleons to purchase and advice on choosing and transporting your chameleon.

1) Preparing Your Home for Your Chameleon

Your veiled chameleon will need a special cage, often called a vivarium. He will spend most of his life in the vivarium, so you do not need to worry about chameleon-proofing your home. This being said, some chameleon owners do give their pets some time outside of the cage to wander. If you choose to do so, follow these steps to make sure your chameleon will remain safe:

- Choose a single room or a smaller area of the house to make safe for your chameleon – if you give him free range of the house there is much more potential for injury, and he may end up hiding someplace where you are unable to find him.

- Make sure the room is secure – your chameleon should not be able to escape and other pets (if you have them) should not be able to enter the room whilst your chameleon is out of his cage.

- Put away all electrical cords and cover open electricity outlets with plastic safety covers.

- Remove all food, cleaning products and other items that could be toxic or harmful to your chameleon, be sure to include any small objects that he might accidentally ingest.

- Make sure the room provides something for your chameleon to climb on - he will feel most comfortable off the ground.

- Never leave your chameleon unsupervised while he is out of his cage – you can allow him to move around freely as long as you keep an eye on him.

- Limit the time your chameleon spends outside his cage – if your chameleon shows sign of becoming stressed with the change in environment, return him to his cage immediately.

Note: Keep in mind that your chameleon does not actually need time out of his cage as long as the cage provides adequate space and it suits his needs. Chameleons are unlikely to be tamed and are perfectly content to remain in their cages for most of their lives. You will read more about handling your veiled chameleon in Chapter Five.

2) Where to Buy Veiled Chameleons

When you are ready to purchase your new pet, do not expect to be able to visit your local pet store and find veiled chameleons for sale. Though veiled chameleons are fairly popular as pets, they are still not the kind of "traditional" pet you would find in most pet stores. This isn't to say that it's impossible, but you need to be prepared to take other measures to locate a veiled chameleon for sale. In this section you will find tips for finding Yemen chameleons in both the U.S. and the U.K.

a) Buying in the U.S.

Even though you might not find one at your local pet store, that doesn't mean it isn't a good place to start to obtain your new pet or to buy veiled chameleon supplies. Ask the store owner if he is aware of any recommended breeders or suppliers that may have a Yemen chameleon for sale – if the store has ever stocked chameleons, the owner will likely have connections. In many cases you would not want to buy a Yemen chameleon from a pet store as you cannot be sure where the chameleon came from, the health of the parents or the conditions in which it was raised.

An ideal way to find veiled chameleons is to attend a reptile trade show. Whether you are looking for an adult or baby veiled chameleon to purchase, this is a good place to find one. Reptile trade shows draw collectors, breeders and dealers of all species of reptiles, so even if you don't find your veiled chameleon, you will likely have made contact with someone who will know where you can look. If you are unable to find a reptile trade show or any local breeders or dealers, your last option may be to check for private sellers. Websites such as Craigslist offer free postings for pets that need to be re-homed, but care must be taken to ensure that you are receiving a chameleon that is in good health.

Links to U.S. Veiled Chameleon Breeders:

FL Chams; www.flchams.com
Backwater Reptiles; www.backwaterreptiles.com
Reptiles by Mack; www.reptilesbymack.com

U.S. Reptile Trade Shows:

Reptiles Magazine; www.reptilesmagazine.com
Kingsnake; www.kingsnake.com
Reptile Super Show; www.reptilesupershow.com

b) Buying in the U.K.

Buying veiled chameleons in the U.K. is very similar to buying in the U.S. You may be able to find a local pet store that has baby veiled chameleons for sale, but you are likely to have to do a little research of your own to find them. Ask local reptile enthusiasts for information about upcoming trade shows or of any recommended experienced breeders. A good place to start may also be by simply performing an online search, you may find a veiled chameleon breeder in your area or at least a community forum where you can gather more information.

Links to U.K. Veiled Chameleon Breeders:

Chameleon Den; www.chameleonden.co.uk
Marcus Langford Reptiles; www.marcus-langford-reptiles.co.uk
Neon Gecko Exotic Pets; www.neongeckoonline.co.uk

U.K. Reptile Trade Shows:

KJ Reptile Supplies; www.kjreptilesupplies.co.uk
Martin Goss; www.martingoss.co.uk
London Pet Show; www.londonpetshow.co.uk

3) Buying a Veiled Chameleon

When you are ready to actually purchase your Yemen chameleon, there are a couple of things you will need to decide. Firstly you should determine whether you want a male or female chameleon and secondly whether you would prefer a juvenile or an adult chameleon. After making these decisions, certain steps should be taken to ensure that you bring home a chameleon that is healthy. Below you will find a list to help with these factors:

- If you do not intend to breed your chameleons, it is best to choose a male. Females can be more difficult to care for due to special needs during egg production.

- Raising juvenile or baby veiled chameleons is generally only recommended for experienced owners, as they are more susceptible to disease if the correct habitat requirements are not met.

- Only purchase captive-bred veiled chameleons – not only is it illegal to buy wild-caught specimens, but they are also more likely to carry parasites and may not do well in captivity.

- Ask to see the chameleons. The breeder or dealer has to offer and perform the following checks:
  - Look for discharge in the eyes, if the eyes are not bright or if the chameleon keeps them closed, it could be a sign of illness.
  - Make sure the chameleon's legs are straight – bowed or bent legs may be a sign of nutritional deficiency or metabolic bone disease.
  - Check the chameleon's feet – he should be able to grip branches firmly and be able to climb with ease.
  - Ensure there are no signs of infection around the mouth, no growths or redness.
  - Check the chameleon's color – the skin should be bright, not patchy or dull.

If you have carried out all these checks and recommendations, there is every probability you will bring home a healthy veiled chameleon.

Note: Avoid purchasing chameleons online and only purchase from experienced and licensed breeders. Purchasing animals online will involve subjecting them to the shipping process during which they may be exposed to severe conditions and rough handling. This is unethical, unfair and could be considered as animal cruelty and therefore should be avoided. Additionally, you would most certainly want to see the veiled chameleon you are purchasing as a pet before you agree to buy.

4) Safely Transporting Your Chameleon

Depending on where you get your chameleon, he may have to endure a lengthy car journey to get him home. For the health and safety of your chameleon, you need to be careful about how you handle and transport him so that he arrives home safely. Travelling can be very stressful for your new chameleon and if he becomes too stressed, it could weaken his immune system and leave him susceptible to illness. Below you will find steps to take to prepare your chameleon for transporting:

1. Select a box for your chameleon to travel in – the box doesn't need to be too large but should have a secure lid that doesn't let in too much light.

2. Use a length of branch to create a perch for your chameleon – push it through the sides of the box a few inches from the bottom so it remains stable.

3. Line the bottom of the box with an old towel in case your chameleon falls off his perch during the trip.

4. Place your chameleon inside the box and close it. As long as the temperature isn't too hot, you do not need

to jab air holes in the box as these will allow unwanted light in.

5. Set the box aside somewhere quiet for at least 30 minutes. Because it will be dark in the box your chameleon will think it's night and hopefully go to sleep.

6. Place the box in the car where it will not move around.

7. Once you arrive at your destination, place your chameleon in his cage and allow him time to adjust.

Note: If you are travelling with your chameleon and the journey will last for several days, bring a temporary cage with you so you can place your chameleon in it when you take a break from your journey. Avoid travelling with your chameleon in a cage or vivarium, placing him in a box is far less stressful and reduces the chances of him falling and injuring himself during the trip.

Visit our website www.VeiledChameleonsCare.com for our contact details or if you are interested in becoming an affiliate for this book.

Chapter Five: Veiled Chameleon Habitat, Feeding and Behavior

As you have already learned, veiled chameleons require a specialized habitat in order to thrive in captivity along with a diet of various insects, supplemented to ensure complete nutrition. In this chapter you will learn how to select and set up your veiled chameleon's cage and suggestions for decorating it to simulate the chameleon's natural habitat. You will learn how to form a diet that will provide for your chameleon's nutritional needs and obtain a sample of a weekly feeding schedule. Finally, you will learn a little more about veiled chameleon behavior including tips for taming and handling your pet.

1) Habitat Requirements

Caring for a veiled chameleon is not something that you should attempt without conducting a great deal of research. As you have already read, the veiled chameleon has very specific needs in regard to its habitat. In the wild, these reptiles come from an area that is naturally warm and humid, so it's this kind of environment you need to replicate in your chameleon's cage. If you do not provide an adequate habitat for your chameleon, he will fail to thrive and could succumb to sickness. In this section you will learn everything you need to know about creating the ideal veiled chameleon environment.

a) Cage Size and Materials

Given the average veiled chameleon size of up to 24 inches (61 cm), you need to be prepared to provide a cage that gives your chameleon plenty of space to move around. When your chameleon is still small, you can safely house him in a standard 10 gallon (38 liter tank). However this will only be adequate until he reaches three months of age. At this stage, a cage that measures at least 16 x 16 x 30 inches (41 x 41 x 72cm) will be required. This cage will be suitable until the chameleon grows to about 8 inches

(20.3cm) long and then he will need to be transferred to his adult cage. There is no harm in keeping a chameleon in a cage larger than he needs, so you may want to save yourself the bother and expense by simply starting out with a cage large enough to house an adult veiled chameleon.

The minimum cage dimensions for an adult veiled chameleon are 2 x 2 x 4 feet (61 x 61 x 122cm), with the largest dimension being the height. Because your chameleon will spend most of his life in this enclosure, you may like to think about having a minimum cage dimension of 3 x 3 x 4 feet (91 x 91 x 122cm) that will provide your chameleon with plenty of space for climbing. Keeping in mind that males are typically larger than females, a male might be best in a cage measuring 3 x 3 x 4 feet (91 x 91 x 122cm) while a female may be perfectly fine in a cage measuring 2 x 2 x 4 feet (61 x 61 x 122cm). Many veiled chameleon owners remark however, that their females are just as active as their males so would most probably appreciate a little extra space.

In addition to choosing the preferred size for your veiled chameleon cage, you also need to choose the right materials. The best cage for a veiled chameleon is a mesh vivarium that will allow for air to flow through the cage whilst ensuring an unimpeded view of your chameleon. Another option is a glass terrarium or fish tank, but this type of cage can often lead to the accumulation of moisture which can subsequently follow on to fungal infections and rot in chameleons. If however you live in a very cold area and have trouble keeping a stable temperature in your Yemen chameleon setup, a glass terrarium may be better for the conservation of heat.

b) Cage Set-up Requirements

After you have chosen your veiled chameleon enclosure, you will now need to begin equipping it. As you are already aware, maintaining the proper temperature and humidity in the cage is of the utmost importance. In order to accomplish this task you will need to install a lighting system using two different types of bulbs - one to provide light and the other heat. In order to provide light, the bulbs to use are UVB – these bulbs simulate natural sunlight that your veiled chameleon requires to be able to properly absorb and utilize nutrients. The lights for heating are often called basking lights and should always be controlled with a thermostat.

To simulate the veiled chameleon's natural environment, you will need to organize your lighting systems to achieve

day and night temperatures. The ideal temperature range for your veiled chameleon during the day is between 75° and 90°F (24° to 32°C) with a basking area reaching between 95° and 105°F (35° to 40°C). Ideally, you should set up your veiled chameleon's cage so that one end is hotter, at least 95°F/35°C, graduating to a cooler temperature of around 75°F/24°C, with mid-range temperatures in between. To achieve this you will need to experiment with your veiled chameleon lighting until the best results in managing the temperatures are reached. In order to monitor the temperature in your veiled chameleon cage you will need to install a thermometer or two although several spaced throughout the cage is an ideal way to monitor the temperature at the hottest end through to the coolest.

To ensure your veiled chameleon is able to bask effectively, make sure the basking lamp at the hottest end of the tank is positioned no more than 6 to 8 inches (15 to 20cm) above the branch where your chameleon will perch. You should also plan to intersperse your basking lamps with UVB lamps so your chameleon has access to both. Do not buy combination heat/UVB lamps because chameleons are able to separately control their body heat and UVB exposure. If your chameleon doesn't get enough UVB light, he will be more susceptible to nutritional deficiencies and metabolic bone disease (MBD).

With regards to how much lighting your chameleon will need, you should expect to keep the lights on for 10 to 12 hours each day. You will however need to check how low the temperature of the cage will drop with all the lights off, but shouldn't need lighting on at night. If you do, be sure to choose a night light as your chameleon may not rest properly if there is light as in the wild, darkness indicates to the chameleon that it is time to sleep. You may wish to consider connecting your lights to an automatic timer, this way you will be able to provide your chameleon with a stable routine without having to worry about remembering to turn lights on or off.

c) Vivarium Accessories

In addition to providing your veiled chameleon with adequate heating and lighting, he will also need objects to climb on. Veiled chameleons are arboreal so will need something tree-like in their enclosure, either artificial plants or simply wooden dowels to simulate branches. Ideally you should use living plants - not only will your chameleon's habitat look more natural but the plants will grow with him and provide an additional food source. Remember, veiled chameleons only drink water droplets from leaves in the wild, so you will also need to replicate this in his vivarium.

You simply cannot use any plants in your vivarium as some houseplants are toxic to chameleons. The most suitable plants to use for your veiled chameleon include hibiscus, ficus and dracaena. These plants can also supplemented with dowels, natural (non-toxic) branches, ropes and vines, thereby equipping your chameleon with an ample climbing system. Remember to position the branches in your chameleon's enclosure so he is able to bask beneath both a heat lamp and a UVB lamp.

You might be wondering what to do with the bottom of your veiled chameleon's cage. Since your chameleon will spend most of his time climbing around, you do not need to worry about using veiled chameleon substrate. However, if you prefer to line the bottom of the vivarium with something to absorb water and waste, use bark or moss. However, you may find that by leaving the bottom of the vivarium bare will make it easier to clean and reduce excess moisture.

d) Cage Maintenance Tasks

Once your chameleon has settled into his enclosure, you will have to maintain it. For the most part, all that is required is to collect and remove waste that will build up in the bottom of the tank. You should also clean and sanitize the walls of the vivarium once a week along with food bowls and other accessories. If you keep the bottom of the vivarium bare, cleaning it will be much simpler by just scooping out the waste and wiping the base clean.

With regards to cleansing your veiled chameleon, these reptiles do not require any kind of bathing or washing. In fact, veiled chameleons do not fare well in and around water (they are not adept for swimming and can actually drown in even small amounts of water). As a rule, your veiled chameleon will stay fairly clean, but if he does become a little dirty, his skin can be cleaned by gently wiping with a damp cloth.

2) Feeding Veiled Chameleon

Aside from ensuring that your veiled chameleon's cage meets his requirements, the most important thing you can do to keep him healthy is to provide him with a nutritious diet. In the wild, these chameleons are primarily insectivorous, although they are likely to eat leaves, blossoms or flowers when other food is scarce. In captivity, insects compose the majority of a veiled chameleon's diet, though many will accept small amounts of fruits and vegetables. It is important to make certain that your chameleon's diet is varied which will help him get a balance of healthy nutrients – if he doesn't, he may suffer from various nutritional deficiencies including metabolic bone disease (MBD). In this section you will learn the basics regarding your chameleon's nutritional needs and tips for formulating a healthy and balanced veiled chameleon diet.

a) Nutritional Needs

Perhaps the most important nutritional need for veiled chameleons is a balance of calcium to phosphorus. Ideally, veiled chameleons need a diet that will provide them with calcium to phosphorus ratio of 2:1. Whilst insects and other foods you offer your chameleon may contain some of these nutrients, it is generally insufficient to provide for his requirements. Consequently you should plan to gut-load your chameleon's feeder insects and dust them with a supplement powder on a regular basis. Gut-loading simply involves supplying your feeder insects with healthy foods so that the nutrients from those foods are passed on to your chameleon when he eats them. Even though gut-loading your feeder insects will go a long way in increasing their nutritional value, you should also aim to use powdered supplements on a regular basis. Check your local pet store or search online for high-quality powdered calcium supplements. To administer the supplement, place your chameleon's daily portion of feeder crickets in a plastic bag, add a pinch of supplement powder and shake the bag until the crickets are coated and then offer them to your chameleon. When he eats them he will be ingesting the supplement powder along with them.

Note: You may want to dust your chameleon's feeder insects only a few times a week to avoid over-supplementation. As you will read further along in this book, too much calcium can be just as dangerous as too little. If you feed your chameleon every day, dust his feeder insects every other feeding.

How To: Sample Gut-Loading Regimen for Insects

If you raise your own feeder insects at home, you should develop some kind of gut-loading regimen to ensure that they provide your chameleon with extra vitamins and minerals. See Appendix B for more information about raising feeder insects at home. Just as you would provide your chameleon with a varied diet, you should also give your feeder insects a variety of foods. Some of the best foods to offer feeder insects include:

- Collard greens
- Kale
- Romaine lettuce
- Carrots
- Sweet potatoes
- Apples
- Squash/zucchini
- Banana skins
- Broccoli
- Alfalfa
- Fish flake food

When raising your own insects at home, you may want to use this sample gut-loading regimen as a feeding guide:

- **Week 1** – collard greens, oranges, fish flake food
- **Week 2** – mustard greens, melon, dried reptile food (crushed)
- **Week 3** – alfalfa pellets (crushed), carrots, dry cat food (crushed)

b) Recommended Types of Foods

As you've already learned, insects form the foundation of a captive Yemen chameleon diet. If you have never owned a reptile before, you may be unaware of just how many options there are when it comes to feeder insects. Below you will find a list of common feeder insects that are best suited for chameleons:

- **Crickets** – these insects are not only easy (and inexpensive) to obtain and raise yourself, but are also easy to gut-load. Crickets offer calcium to phosphorus ratio of 1:1 so should be dusted with calcium supplements often. Crickets are also a good source of protein.

- **Mealworms** – these insects come in a variety of sizes and can also be gut-loaded like crickets. Mealworms are beetle larvae, so raising your own will give you an endless renewing supply.

- **Wax worms** – these insects are also called grubs and are a favorite of chameleons. Wax worms are high in fat content and should be gut-loaded to increase their nutritional value.

- **Grasshoppers** – these insects are also a favorite of chameleons, but are not as easy to obtain or raise as other feeder insects. Not only are they larger than crickets, but grasshoppers are also "meatier". If you gather them yourself, do so in an area that has not been treated with pesticides or insecticides.

- **Silkworms** – these insects are plump and juicy and loved by chameleons when they can get them. If allowed to pupate, silkworms will turn into moths that will also make a good food for your chameleon.

- **Hornworms** – both tomato and tobacco hornworms are viable options as feeder insects for chameleons. These worms are large and plump but not so easily obtainable as other foods – you may need to order them online.

- **Flies** – though flies form a significant portion of the wild chameleon's diet, there are many more nutritious options for captive chameleons.

- **Roaches** – though you may not like the idea of keeping cockroaches in your house, they are an excellent source of nutrition for chameleons. Roaches breed quickly providing you with an endless supply, and as long as you buy the kind that cannot climb glass or plastic walls (Madagascar hissing cockroach), you will have no worries about them escaping into your house.

Your chameleon may not eat it regularly, but it wouldn't hurt to offer some fresh fruit and vegetables once in a while. Some non-insect foods your chameleon may accept include:

- Dandelion greens
- Collard greens
- Kale
- Escarole
- Endive
- Carrots
- Squash

- Sweet potatoes
- Red bell peppers
- Pears
- Apple
- Melon
- Berries

Note: Not all veiled chameleons will accept fruits and vegetables. In the wild, these foods are typically only eaten when water is not readily available. In captivity, fruits and vegetables do not form a significant part of the veiled chameleon's diet, so you shouldn't be worried if he or she rejects them.

How To: Foods to Avoid Overfeeding

You already know the importance of offering your chameleon a variety of insects, but you need to be aware, that certain insects should only be presented in moderation. Crickets are a great all-purpose feeder for veiled chameleons and can make up the majority of his insect diet. There are other insects however that should be fed sparingly. Below you will find a list of insects that you should only feed occasionally and why:

- **Wax worms** – these insects have low calcium to phosphorus level; they are also very high in fat compared to other insects.

- **Meal worms** - these insects have low calcium to phosphorus level in comparison to others.

- **King worms** – these worms have likely been fed growth hormones to increase their size and could be dangerous for your chameleon.

- **Fruit flies** – these insects are best for veiled chameleon hatchlings only; they can quickly multiple and infest the chameleon's vivarium.

- **Houseflies** – fairly low in nutrition compared to other feeder insect options.

Note: You should also avoid feeding your chameleon any insect that is larger than the width of his head because he may have trouble swallowing it.

c) Tips for Feeding Chameleons

While your veiled chameleon is still growing, you should aim to feed him as much as he is willing to eat, on a daily basis. Once he matures however, you may want to reduce his feeding routine to every other day. It will be for you to decide how much you feed your chameleon and it will also depend on how much he tends to eat. Some chameleon owners feed their adults between 12 and 24 crickets (or similar sized feeder insects) at each feeding whilst others simply offer as much as the chameleon will eat during a 30 minute period. By offering your chameleon several insects at one time until he stops eating, will avoid the hassle of having to collect the uneaten insects.

The method you choose to offer insects to your veiled chameleon is entirely up to you. You will have difficulty containing certain insects such as crickets, so they are best offered free-roaming. For worms, such as wax worms and mealworms however, you might want to offer them in a shallow dish preventing them from crawling under anything before your chameleon can eat them. Use a opaque or semi-opaque feeder cup with the insects inside and place the cup inside the cage for your chameleon to eat from. Many chameleon owners use a combination of these two methods, so you can experiment to see what will work best for you and your chameleon. However if you want to promote natural hunting behaviors for your veiled chameleon, use the free-roaming technique.

How To: Sample Weekly Feeding Schedule

Over time you will establish which insects your chameleon prefers and you will be able to formulate a specialized feeding schedule around them. When you are first starting out however, you may find it helpful to have a template to begin with. Below you will find a sample weekly feeding schedule for an adult veiled chameleon:

- **Sunday** – 12 to 20 gut-loaded crickets (dusted with calcium supplement powder).

- **Monday** – nothing.

- **Tuesday** – 6 to 8 gut-loaded mealworms, 3 to 4 gut-loaded cockroaches (dusted with calcium supplement powder).

- **Wednesday** – nothing.

- **Thursday** – 12 to 20 gut-loaded crickets (dusted with calcium supplement powder).

- **Friday** – nothing.

- **Saturday** – 4 to 5 wax worms, 6 to 8 gut-loaded mealworms (dusted with calcium supplement powder).

Note: Keep in mind that even on days when you do not feed your veiled chameleon, you will still need to mist the cage for 1 to 2 minutes to provide him with drinking water.

3) Veiled Chameleon Behavior

Even though no training or experience is required in owning a veiled chameleon, it will take you sometime to become accustomed to caring for this unique pet. Because veiled chameleons are wild animals that have been bred in captivity for the pet industry, you should not expect them to act like traditional pets. If you truly want to provide the best environment possible for your chameleon, you will need to learn not only about his habitat requirements, but also about his behavior. The more you know about chameleon behavior, the better you will become at being able to understand your pet. In this section you will learn about common behavior in chameleons and what it means. You will also receive tips for handling and taming your chameleon.

a) Common Behaviors and What They Mean

The first thing you need to know about veiled chameleon behavior is that these animals are very shy by nature. If your chameleon starts to behave erratically or in any extreme way, it could be a sign that something is wrong and you need to seek veterinary advice as soon as possible.

Below you will find a list of normal chameleon behaviors as well as an explanation as to what they may mean:

- **Dark color change** – often indicates stress, illness, or temperature being too low.

- **Abnormally light color** – may indicate stress, illness, or temperature too high.

- **Vivid coloration** – territorial display or stress.

- **Walking slowly while rocking** – normal behavior, meant to mimic a branch in the wind.

- **Gaping and/or hissing** – defensive display, may indicate fear.

- **Swiveling eyes** – normal behavior and being watchful for predators and potential prey.

b) Handling Your Chameleon Correctly

Even though some pet reptiles such as ball pythons and leopard geckos respond very well to handling, this is not always the case with veiled chameleons. More often than not for a veiled chameleon, being held can be very stressful.

How well a chameleon responds to contact will depend on his individual temperament. If your chameleon reacts poorly or obviously becomes stressed by the experience, you should respect him and handle him as little as possible. In most cases however, veiled chameleons will tolerate short periods of handling.

How To: Introducing Yourself to Your Chameleon

When you bring your chameleon home for the first time, he is likely to be very overwhelmed by the change in environment. Do not plan to handle your chameleon for several days after you place him in his new vivarium, ideally one to two weeks after you bring him home. It is normal for a chameleon to refuse food for the first several days of this transition, but as he becomes more comfortable with his surroundings, he will start to exhibit normal behaviors including a healthy appetite.

When the time comes to introduce yourself to your chameleon, you will need to be mindful as to how you go about it - you always want your chameleon to associate being handled with good things. Forcing him to come out of his cage before he is ready will not be a good start, but coaxing him out may be the answer. One thing you might try is leaving the cage door open and sitting nearby holding a ficus tree just outside the cage for your chameleon to climb onto. When the chameleon is ready, he will come out of the cage and look around, which may take time at first and a lot of patience from you, but eventually your chameleon may be eager to come out and explore.

Once your chameleon is used to coming out of his cage, begin offering your hand as an extension of the tree for him to climb on. If your chameleon doesn't appear to be afraid or stressed, you may even be able to lift him carefully from the tree and place him on your hand or arm. Hold your chameleon for about a minute and then place him back onto the tree. Over time you can gradually increase the duration of handling, but never force it on your chameleon for longer than he is comfortable.

c) Taming and Training Your Chameleon

Although you should never expect your chameleon to become completely tame, over time you may be able to train him to eat food out of your hand (with regards to a chameleon, this is as tame as he is likely to get). The first steps to take in taming a veiled chameleon are the same as those outlined in the previous section, firstly get your chameleon accustomed to coming out of his cage and then being handled for short periods of time. Once he is contented to be handled regularly you can start training him to eat food from your hand.

Start by allowing the chameleon to climb around freely then place your open palm in front of him within his view. Put a wax worm in the palm of your hand, keeping your hand very still, until he takes the worm from your palm with his tongue. It may take a few attempts for your chameleon to accept the food, but if he has been tamed enough to handle, he should be receptive. If you start your chameleon with this kind of training while he is still young, he will grasp it more quickly.

Chapter Six: Breeding Veiled Chameleons

Breeding Yemen chameleons in captivity is not especially difficult, but that doesn't mean you should attempt it without carefully considering all the details. Unlike some pets, veiled chameleons can produce dozens of babies at any one time, so you need to think about whether you will be able to care for so many chameleons at once. If you decide that breeding veiled chameleons is something you would like to do, or if you just want to learn more about the process, in this chapter you will find information about how to breed veiled chameleons, including everything from basic breeding information and care for female chameleons, to specifics such as creating a nesting box and incubating the eggs.

1) Understanding How Chameleons Breed

The decision to breed veiled chameleons is not one that should be made lightly, not only do you need to provide housing for two adult chameleons, but you also need to care for the veiled chameleon babies once they hatch. It is important to note that the reproductive cycle can be very taxing on the female, potentially shortening her lifespan by several years if she produces clutches on a regular basis. If however you have decided to breed your chameleons, start by equipping yourself with as much information about the process. This will enable you to attempt it in the correct way and with plenty of confidence.

The veiled chameleon is an oviparous breeder – this simply means they produce and lay eggs rather than give birth to live, already developed young. The male of the species can reach sexual maturity as early as 4 to 5 months of age while females usually take a little longer, approx 6 months. For the safety of your chameleons, you should wait until they are at least 8 (20 cm), ideally 12 inches (30.5 cm) for males, in length before you attempt to breed them. You should also keep in mind that male and female veiled chameleons should not be housed together – they should only be introduced for short periods of time solely for the purpose of breeding.

You should not assume that your chameleons will be ready to breed at any time, there are signs to look out for which will indicate that the female is ready to accept the male. The most obvious sign will be her color. When a female veiled chameleon is ready for breeding, she will exhibit a neutral coloration, but to be sure she is ready, introduce the male and female and see how they react. If the female maintains her coloration and nonchalantly ignores the male perhaps by walking away from him, it means that she is receptive. If the female is non-receptive she will likely turn black and start rocking back and forth. The female may also gape, puff out her throat or run away from the male.

If the female does appear receptive, you can leave her in the male's cage until they breed. In most cases mating will occur within a few minutes of the introduction, although it can take several hours. Nevertheless, be sure to watch your chameleons closely in the event that something doesn't go to plan. The actual mating process of veiled chameleons can take anywhere between 10 and 45 minutes, but you should be prepared to leave the two together for 24 to 48 hours as long as there are no problems, until a successful mating is achieved. You will know when the female is inseminated because she will turn black, often with green and yellow spots. When you become aware of this, it is time to separate the two sexes.

After the female is inseminated, she will go through a gestation period lasting between 3 to 5 weeks. During this time the female will start to swell as the eggs grow within her, but her intake of food may not increase significantly. The size of the female will depend on the size of the clutch – the average size for a veiled chameleon clutch is between 12 and 20 eggs. For the sake of your female's health, you should hope for a clutch on the lower end of the spectrum as large clutches tend to be particularly taxing on your female and may result in a shortened lifespan.

Whilst the female veiled chameleon is gravid (pregnant) her size will increase, particularly near the back of the torso. You should not increase your female's food supply significantly during this period, but you should be sure to supplement her diet to ensure she gets enough calcium for the eggs. As the pregnancy progresses the female will start to become restless and may start pacing around the cage looking for a site to lay her eggs. By the 20th day after conception you should prepare and offer a nesting box. If you do not provide an adequate site for your female to lay her eggs, she will retain them and as a result may become egg bound.

2) Caring for Female Veiled Chameleons

If you have never owned a female reptile before, you may be surprised when your female veiled chameleon lays eggs. Even if your female chameleon never comes into contact with a male, she will still produce and lay eggs throughout the year. In the wild veiled chameleons may only mate once each year, but are capable of breeding several times a year in captivity as long as they are provided with the right conditions. One aspect of caring for a female veiled chameleon will involve providing her with the opportunity to develop and deliver eggs.

A female veiled chameleon is capable of producing eggs as young as 6 months of age. Males on the other hand, may mature earlier. For the safety of your female chameleon however, you should avoid breeding her until she is at least 8 inches (20 cm) long. With or without a male, female veiled chameleons will generally lay eggs every few months. The eggs will develop over a period of 3 to 5 weeks and once they are laid, the female will rest for a few months before going through the entire process again. Unfortunately, this process is incredibly taxing on the female's body so you can expect a female veiled chameleon to have a shorter lifespan than a male – it may be as low as half the lifespan of a male chameleon.

Although you cannot stop your female from producing and laying eggs (nor should you), there are certain things you can do to ensure that the process does not become too stressful or dangerous for her health. The most important tasks you can undertake for your female veiled chameleon is to monitor her feeding and be observant of the temperature in her vivarium. In the wild, an abundance of food and warm temperatures is a signal that the conditions are ideal for reproduction. Hence, if you hope to prolong your chameleon's life by reducing the number of clutches she has, you should avoid overfeeding her and keep the temperature a little lower than you would for a male veiled chameleon.

During the period your female veiled chameleon is growing, you should feed her as much as you would a male juvenile, normally as much as she will eat during a 10 to 15-minute period of time. By the time she reaches 5 ½ to 6 months old however, you should start to lessen her feedings to a maximum of 8 to 12 crickets (or the equivalent to other feeder insects) every other day. This feeding schedule will enable your female to maintain growth but at a steadier pace, signaling her body not to start producing eggs too soon. In order to really slow your chameleon's metabolism however, you must make adjustments to the temperature in her enclosure.

The maximum temperature in your female veiled chameleon's cage (the basking temperature) should be about 83°F (28°C). The ambient temperature in the tank should be just a few degrees lower than you would normally keep it – about 75°F (24°C) at the high end and in the mid to high 60s at night-time. Maintaining a lower temperature in your female's cage will slow down her metabolism, which will in turn, slow her reproductive cycle. Your female will still produce and lay eggs, but the clutches will likely be smaller and may also be less frequent.

3) Setting Up a Nesting Box

A nesting box for veiled chameleon breeding doesn't need to be grand. A bucket or bin full of moist sand in which your female chameleon can dig is quite sufficient. In the wild, female chameleons may spend days looking for the ideal nesting site and then dig a deep hole over a period of several hours in which to lay their eggs. In captivity however, all you need to do for your female is to provide an opaque container filled with at least 12 inches (30.5 cm) of moist sand or organic soil. The bin should be no less than 8 inches (20.3 cm) wide so she has enough room to turn around comfortably.

When the female starts to appear restless and it is nearing the time when her clutch is due, place the nesting box in the cage where she can find it. Though your female will likely reduce her intake of food and water during this time, you should still continue to offer it. When she is ready, the female will dig a hole about 3 inches (7.6cm) wide, angling it to a depth of 4 to 8 inches (10 to 20.3cm). Your female may dig several holes in the bin, but she will lay all her eggs in just one. If you notice the female digging multiple holes, it could mean that the substrate is too moist for her liking. If the conditions are right she will deposit her eggs, cover them over and resume normal activity – she will not play any role in raising the veiled chameleon babies after this time.

How To: If Your Female is Reluctant to Lay

If your female veiled chameleon is reluctant to lay her eggs even after you have provided a nesting box, you may need to make some adjustments. Some veiled chameleons do not like to lay eggs in a nesting box that contains only soil. In the event that this may be the problem, you might consider mixing the soil with sand. Another option is to place a small plant in a corner of the box to make her feel more comfortable. If the female simply refuses to lay her eggs and you are sure that the conditions are adequate, you may need to entrap her in a container and keep her there until she deposits her eggs. To do this, use a tall kitchen garbage can, or something similar, filled with 12 inches (30.5cm) of substrate and a few small branches.

Eventually, the female should begin to dig and will lay her eggs. If she still refuses to dig, try again the next day. Avoid checking on her too often as this might distract her, instead leaving her alone for most of the day ensuring she is in a warm and quiet area. You do not need to cover the bin too securely if it is too tall for her to escape, but draping a cloth over the top may help her to feel more comfortable. If the female still refuses to lay her eggs and starts to show symptoms of being egg bound, seek veterinary care immediately for what could rapidly become a fatal condition.

4) Incubating the Eggs

Once your female Yemen chameleon lays her eggs, her
motherly duty is done – she will take no part in raising the
hatchlings. If you carefully push aside the substrate in the
nesting box, you will find somewhere between 10 and 80
little white eggs each containing a Yemen chameleon baby
that will develop over the forthcoming months. Yemen
chameleon eggs take between 6 and 13 months to develop,
although 8 to 10 months is average. The development
period is long, so you will need to make sure that you have
a safe place to keep the eggs while they incubate.

Incubating your chameleon's eggs is not difficult, but there
are a few basic guidelines you should follow. Choose a
deep plastic container with a capacity of at least 16 ounces
(0.5 liter) with a tight-fitting lid. Keep in mind that the
deeper the container, the easier it will be to maintain the
humidity inside. Fill the container with several inches of
vermiculite (regular or coarse grade) that is moistened with
distilled water at a ratio of 1:1 water to vermiculite. Spread
the vermiculite in the incubation box and carefully place
the eggs in even rows about 1 to 1.5 inches (2.5 to 3.8cm)
deep, spacing them at least 1 inch apart. Make sure there is
a clearance of several inches between the top of the

vermiculite and the lid of the container, which will allow you to see the chameleons once they hatch.

After transferring the eggs to the incubation box, place it in a dark place where it will not be disturbed for the next 8 to 10 months. The exact temperature of the location is not important, but should be maintained between 73° and 80°F (23° to 27°C). Check the box every month to make sure the vermiculite is still moist. If you find that any of the eggs have turned black or shriveled, you can remove them from the box. As long as everything goes well, you can expect your veiled chameleon babies to emerge after 8 to 10 months - in some cases more and others less.

5) Raising the Hatchlings

As the end of the incubation period approaches, you may notice the eggs starting to swell and a crosshatching pattern may also appear on the shell. After 6 months, begin to check the eggs more frequently and look for signs of hatching. The first indication that the eggs are getting ready to hatch is when they start to sweat. Next a star-shaped pattern will appear at one end of the egg – this is the mark of the baby Yemen chameleon breaking the shell from the inside. Shortly thereafter you will see a slit forming in the egg and the release of its internal fluids.

As the eggs continue to hatch, you may see them start to collapse. It will generally take a few hours from the time the slit appears in the egg to when the hatchling is free. Do not be alarmed if the hatchlings rest for a time after they emerge - the shorter the rest period the stronger the hatchling is. You may also find that some of the eggs do not hatch even after the slit appears – the babies in those eggs simply weren't strong enough to complete the process. This is normal and unless a large percentage or the whole of the clutch died, you should not be concerned. Within a few hours of hatching, the baby chameleons should be climbing around the box, covered in damp vermiculite.

Once the babies have hatched, you can house them in 10 gallon (38 liter) tanks in groups of 6 to 8. Make sure to cover the top of the tanks to prevent the hatchlings from escaping. It is also recommended that you provide plenty of small plants and branches for climbing and maintain a daytime temperature between 88° and 95° (31° to 35°C) with night-time temperatures falling to approx 75° to 80°F (24° to 26°C). It is essential that you mist the cage often to keep the humidity up and to provide the hatchlings with water to drink.

At this stage you may be wondering what to feed the hatchlings. Feeding baby veiled chameleon hatchlings is no different from feeding adults, you just have to use smaller insects. Pinhead crickets are ideal for hatchlings and you are at liberty to offer as many as the hatchlings will want to eat. Be sure to dust the crickets with calcium powder to make sure the baby's bones develop properly. When the hatchlings get to be about 2 months old, plan to divide the sexes and separate them into larger cages. If possible keep the males in individual cages out of sight of each other, but the females may be able to be kept together for a little while longer. Once the hatchlings are 2 months old you can start to find and place them in their new homes, unless of course, you plan to keep them all!

Chapter Seven: Veiled Chameleon Health and Hygiene

The key to keeping your veiled chameleon healthy, is to provide him with a suitable habitat and a nutritious diet. However even after providing these essentials, there is always the possibility of your chameleon falling ill. The best way to protect your chameleon is to learn the basics about common illnesses affecting this species and how to recognize and treat them. In this chapter you will learn about potential health problems for veiled chameleons as well as common injuries and advice for correct hygiene procedures for your chameleon tank and after handling him.

1) Health Problems Affecting Chameleons

As long as you provide your chameleon with a healthy diet and a habitat that fulfils his requirements, he should remain fairly healthy. When you fail to perform routine maintenance tasks in cleaning the cage, or if you let the standards of your chameleon's diet fall, he is likely to become ill. However, even if you are taking excellent care of your chameleon, there is always the possibility that he could become sick from contaminated food, stress or other factors. The key for ensuring that your chameleon makes a full recovery will lie in your ability to identify the problem and treat it correctly.

In this section you will learn about some of the conditions and health problems veiled chameleons are likely to suffer. You will receive information about the cause of these problems as well as the symptoms to look out for and potential treatment options. The purpose in providing this information is to familiarize you with potential problems so you can identify them quickly and get your chameleon the care he needs as soon as possible.

Some potential health problems affecting the veiled chameleon breed include:

- Burns
- Dehydration
- Egg Binding
- Eye Problems
- Kidney Failure
- Metabolic Bone Disease
- Upper Respiratory Infection
- Stomatitis

Note: The information in this chapter is not intended to serve as a replacement for veterinary care, it is only to help you identify problems if they occur. If you suspect that your chameleon is sick, take note of his symptoms, when they started and seek veterinary advice as soon as possible.

Burns

Though veiled chameleons enjoy warm temperatures and the ability to bask, they can be burned if they get too close to a heat source. Thermal burns are the result of a chameleon coming into direct contact with a heat source or simply by being too close to heat, for example with ceramic heaters. If you choose to use a ceramic heater, be sure to place it outside the vivarium so your chameleon doesn't come into contact with it. Ensure basking lamps are positioned at least 6 inches (15cm) above the highest perch. You should also be wary of setting lamps directly on top of the cage, especially if the cage is mesh – your chameleon may climb up the mesh and burn himself.

Thermal burns firstly appear on chameleons as the area turning white, after this the chameleon may resume his normal habits, but that doesn't mean you should avoid taking him to the vet. Burns can quickly progress to a black color and will then form a scab. After this happens the tissue will become necrotic and peel off, leaving a pink colored scar underneath. With severe burns and tissue loss, infection is a real concern. Even after the wound has healed, the scarring is likely to be permanent. If you even suspect that your chameleon has been burned, take him to the vet immediately.

Dehydration

You have already read about veiled chameleons only drinking water in droplet form from plants in their enclosure. Given this information, it is understandable dehydration might be a common problem, especially if you do not mist your chameleon's enclosure frequently. Unfortunately it can be difficult to recognize the sign of dehydration in chameleons until it has become very severe. Even minor dehydration over a long period of time can be dangerous, and sometimes fatal for chameleons.

Some of the signs of dehydration in chameleons include sunken eyes, yellow or orange urine, loss of appetite, lethargy and skin not returning to normal position after pinching. When detected early, dehydration can be treated very easily by showering your chameleon. Simply place an artificial plant in your bathtub and adjust the showerhead so that the spray rebounds off the wall allowing the reflected water to hit the plant. Place your chameleon in the plant and let him shower (supervised) for 30 to 45 minutes. It may require two sessions each day over a period of several days until your chameleon is fully hydrated.

The showering method of rehydration is only recommended when your chameleon is reaching dangerous levels of dehydration. For minor levels you may be able to simply mist the cage several times a day and watch over your chameleon to make sure he is drinking.

Egg Binding

Also referred to as egg retention or dystocia, egg binding occurs when a gravid female chameleon is unwilling or unable to lay her eggs. In many cases, this results from a failure on the owner's part to provide an adequate nesting box. In other cases however, it may be the result of excess stress, poor nutrition or malformed or fused eggs. The key to preventing this condition is to provide a gravid female with a suitable nesting box after the 20th day of pregnancy.

When your chameleon is nearing the end of her gestation, monitor her behavior. She should show interest in the nesting box by digging around to test the substrate. If your chameleon reaches her due date and hasn't deposited the eggs, and she's becoming increasingly restless, you need to seek veterinary care immediately. This is especially important if the chameleon appears to be in pain or if dehydration becomes an issue. Unless the eggs are removed, the chameleon is in danger of dying within 24 hours.

When you take your chameleon to the vet, he is likely to administer a calcium injection along with oxytocin to induce egg laying. This treatment is usually effective within the hour. If 3 doses over a 24-hour period do not result in egg laying, the removal of the eggs by surgery is the only remaining option.

Eye Problems

Because veiled chameleons have protruding eyes, they seem to be more vulnerable to eye problems than other reptiles. Not only are they susceptible to eye injuries, but also to infections, foreign bodies and other problems. Firstly the most easily treated eye problem is a foreign body inside the eye turret, this may be something such as a piece of soil or bark that has lodged in the eye. Symptoms of this condition may include signs of discomfort, bulging eye, rubbing of the eye on objects or scratching it. If you think something is in your chameleon's eye, a prolonged misting or shower may help to dislodge it. If the problem persists seek veterinary care.

Another potential cause of eye problems in chameleons is over-exposure to UVB. This is particularly common in vivariums where coil-shaped UVB bulbs are used. Avoid placing your UVB bulbs in the same area where your heat bulbs are as your chameleon could become overexposed to UVB whilst basking. Avoid the temptation to use combination heat/UVB bulbs in your vivarium.

Vitamin A deficiency is a third cause of eye problems. Vitamin A is fat-soluble and plays an essential role in the chameleon's metabolism. Without it, you may notice that the chameleon's eyes swell or they draw up inside the head. If you suspect vitamin A deficiency, administering very small doses of preformed vitamin A may help but you should ideally seek veterinary care as too much vitamin A can cause toxicity.

Kidney Failure

Also referred to as renal disease, kidney failure in chameleons is typically the result of chronic low-level dehydration. When the chameleon is subjected to inadequate watering methods or low humidity in the vivarium for extended periods of time, a great deal of stress is put upon the kidneys, which will eventually lead to failure. Some of the most common signs of renal disease in chameleons include loss of appetite, depression, weight loss, lethargy and weakness. If the condition is allowed to progress, it may lead to gular edema and sunken eyes.

Proper hydration is the best way to prevent kidney failure in captive chameleons. Not only do you need to mist your chameleon's cage frequently, but you should also monitor him to be certain he is drinking regularly. For emergency hydration, you may be able to mist the chameleon in the shower – see the section on Dehydration for more information regarding this method. As long as the chameleon is rehydrated it can recover from this condition. It is important however to monitor the chameleon's hydration thereafter to prevent recurrence.

Metabolic Bone Disease

Unfortunately metabolic bone disease (MBD) is fairly common in veiled chameleons and other pet reptiles. This disease is very complex, so a variety of factors make up its development. Generally the main cause is lack of calcium or vitamin D3 in the diet. It may also develop as a result of improper calcium to phosphorus ratio in the diet. The easiest way to prevent this disease is to gut-load your feeder insects as a general rule, and to dust your chameleon's insects with powdered supplements several times a week – this will prevent deficiencies.

The effects of metabolic bone disease can be subtle at first, although can compound with time and become very dangerous. At first, your chameleon may become lethargic and lose his appetite until eventually you may notice deformities in his legs – they may start to assume a U-shape more so than the ideal 90 degree bend. In some cases MBD affects the chameleon's ability to control his tongue, he may have trouble grabbing food or projecting/retracting his tongue entirely. In extreme cases MBD may result in spinal deformities or "kinks". If left untreated, MBD as a rule will result in death, especially in juveniles. If you suspect that your chameleon is suffering from MBD seek veterinary care immediately.

Upper Respiratory Infection

One of the most common health problems in veiled chameleons is the upper respiratory infection (URI). This condition is usually a direct result of poor hygiene. In many cases it is the result of accumulation of waste and water on the bottom of the cage, although it can also develop when the temperature in the enclosure is too low or the humidity too high. Allowing the air in the enclosure to become stagnant, can also be a contributory factor for upper respiratory infections in chameleons.

The infection itself is caused by bacteria that manifests in either the respiratory tract or the sinuses. If left untreated, the infection can spread to the lungs and cause pneumonia. When this happens, aggressive treatment is required and the chameleon may not make a full recovery. Common symptoms of respiratory infections include gaping, stringy mucus inside the mouth, raspy breathing, wheezing, inflammation around the nostrils and bubbling at the mouth and nose.

Unfortunately early symptoms of this condition can be easily missed, which is why you need to seek veterinary care as soon as you suspect a URI. Raising the temperature in the vivarium may help and your vet is likely to prescribe a broad-spectrum antibiotic. With proper treatment, these infections usually clear up within 4 to 10 days.

Stomatitis

Also known as mouth rot, stomatitis is unfortunately fairly common in captive reptiles including the veiled chameleon. Stomatitis is actually a bacterial infection, even though the name "mouth rot" might imply a fungal infection. This condition can affect the gums, palate and tongue of the chameleon that will eventually affect its ability to eat, which makes it a very dangerous condition if left untreated. In the early stages, symptoms of stomatitis may include discoloring of the gum line or brown matter forming around the teeth and gums. Your chameleon might also develop an overbite if the lower jaw begins to swell.

If you notice abnormalities in the shape of your chameleon's mouth, or if you see visible evidence of infection, take him to the vet as soon as possible. If you do not treat this condition quickly, it can invade the mouth and even the jawbone and the damage from this level of infection may be irreparable. Treatment for this condition usually involves antibiotic treatment. For severe cases where the infection has invaded the teeth or bones, surgery may be required to remove the infected teeth. In some cases, stomatitis can be a secondary infection resulting from trauma to the inside of the mouth such as a cut or scratch.

2) Maintaining Proper Hygiene

It is important not only for your chameleon's health, but also for your own, that you maintain proper hygiene. Although you are unlikely to contract a disease as a direct result of handling your chameleon, there is always the possibility of bacteria being transmitted from your chameleon to you. There are also certain diseases or conditions to which your chameleon may be more susceptible if you fail to enact certain hygiene procedures. Below you will find an overview of common hygiene related problems and tips for maintaining good hygiene for and around your chameleon:

Chameleon Hygiene Checklist

You should spend several minutes each day observing your veiled chameleon for signs of good health. The more time you spend getting to know your chameleon's normal appearance and behavior, the more quickly you will be able to detect a problem should it arise. Some points to look for during your routine hygiene checks are:

- Healthy-looking skin, normal coloration.
- Eyes are clear and free of discharge.
- No excessive scratching or rubbing.
- Mouth is clean and free of rot or growths.

- The tail is healthy and free from damage.
- Normal eating, drinking and waste elimination.
- No signs of diarrhea in the cage.
- Area under the tail is relatively clean (no sign of diarrhea).

Basic Vivarium Hygiene

Keeping your chameleon's vivarium clean is essential for his health. Perform these basic hygiene procedures:

- If you are providing a bowl of water, change it daily.
- If you use substrate, refresh it every few days and replace it entirely once a week.
- Remove any uneaten food (especially fruit and vegetables) within 1 hour to prevent decay.
- Wipe down and sanitize the vivarium walls and bottom at least once a week.
- Always use fresh water when misting your chameleon's cage.

Preventing Salmonella

Salmonella is a form of bacteria that can be transmitted from reptiles to humans. Your risk of contracting salmonella is greater if you fail to follow basic hygiene principles such as these:

- Always wash your hands thoroughly before and after handling your veiled chameleon.

- Avoid touching your mouth or face until you have washed your hands.

- Keep accessories from your chameleon's cage away from the kitchen area to prevent transmission of bacteria to food.

- Keep antibacterial hand wash near the vivarium so you can wash your hands before touching anything else in the house.

- If your chameleon bites you, clean the wound thoroughly and cover with a bandage until fully healed.

3) Common Injuries for Chameleons

In addition to equipping yourself with knowledge regarding common health problems affecting the veiled chameleon and being aware of proper hygiene procedures, you may also want to familiarize yourself with common injuries your chameleon may sustain. Below you will find an overview of injuries that your chameleon might receive along with tips on how to handle them:

- **Open Wounds** – these could result from a sharp object in the cage or could be sustained during a breeding session. Wounds should be thoroughly cleaned with warm water and mild antibacterial soap. If the wound is deep, seek veterinary care as soon as possible.

- **Cuts and Scratches** – superficial wounds such as shallow cuts and scratches could occur as your chameleon moves around the cage, especially if there are sharp edges or cut branches. Clean the wound with water and antibacterial soap then apply a thin layer of antiseptic ointment and leave the wound uncovered.

- **Eye Injury** – because the chameleon's eyes protrude from its head, they are prone to injury. If your chameleon's eye is injured you may want to flush it with water but seek veterinary care immediately to prevent further damage or infection.

- **Skeletal Deformities** – if you notice a deformity in your chameleon's spine or limbs, you may at first think that it is a break, possibly the result of a fall. More likely, it is due to a nutritional deficiency such as MBD. Seek veterinary care immediately.

- **Tail Loss** – unlike many reptiles, chameleons do not have tail autonomy (they cannot voluntarily drop their tail to escape a predator). If your chameleon loses his tail it should be considered a serious injury and should be taken to the vet immediately. This is unlikely to happen unless he is exposed to another chameleon and they fight or if it gets an infection.

a) First Aid Kit for Chameleons

Although you are unlikely to have to perform any kind of major wound care for your chameleon, it's best to be prepared. If you allow your chameleon out of his cage once in a while, there is a greater chance of him hurting himself.

There is also the possibility that he might fall in the cage and suffer from a minor injury. In cases such as these, you will be relieved that you have prepared yourself with basic first aid knowledge for reptiles. It is also sensible to have a reptile first aid kit stocked with the following items:

- Betadine - to disinfect.
- Assorted needles and syringes.
- Eye dropper.
- Clippers - for claws.
- First aid paper tape - adheres to reptile skin.
- Gauze sponges.
- Sterile bandages in assorted sizes.
- Cotton swabs.
- Mild antibacterial soap.
- Triple antiseptic ointment.
- Pedialyte - for emergency hydration.
- Sterile saline - to flush wounds.
- Styptic powder - stops minor wounds bleeding.
- Latex gloves.
- Small flashlight.
- Magnifying glass.
- Tweezers.

Note: Keep your first aid kit in a convenient location close to your chameleon's cage for easy access when needed. If you are traveling carry the first aid kit with you.

Chapter Eight: Veiled Chameleon Care Sheet

Even though you will find information relating to veiled chameleons throughout this book, there may come a time when you need to reference a certain fact quickly. Rather than having to leaf through the whole book or re-read an entire chapter, check these care sheets for the information you need. Here you will find the most important veiled chameleon facts in the following categories:

- Species Information
- Vivarium Set-up and Requirements
- Feeding and Nutritional Needs
- Information about Breeding

1) Species Information

- The scientific name for the veiled chameleon is *Chamaeleo calyptratus.*
- Also known as the Yemen chameleon, the veiled chameleon is one of over 150 chameleon species in its genus.
- Veiled chameleons are found primarily in the mountainous regions of Yemen, although they also live in Saudi Arabia and the United Arab Emirates.
- This species is omnivorous, though feed mainly on insects.
- Unique physical attributes of this species include a helmet-like casque, zygodactylous feet, a prehensile tail and swivel eyes.
- Males are both larger and more colorful than females.
- The average size for a male veiled chameleon is 17 to 24 inches (43 to 61cm) long, weighing 3.5 to 7 ounces (100 to 200g).
- The average size for a female is 10 to 14 inches (25 to 35.5cm) long, weighing 3.2 to 4.2 ounces (90 to 120g).
- Male veiled chameleons are bright green with patches or stripes of blue, yellow or brown color.

- Females of the species are dull green, exhibiting blue or yellow spots during breeding.
- The average veiled chameleon lifespan is around 5 years.

2) Vivarium Set-up and Requirements

- A baby veiled chameleon can be housed in a standard 10 gallon (38 liter) tank until 3 months old.
- A juvenile needs a cage measuring at least 16 x 16 x 30 inches (41 x 41 x 72cm).
- When the juvenile reaches 8 inches (20.3cm) he must be transferred to his adult cage.
- The minimum cage dimensions for an adult veiled chameleon are 2 x 2 x 4 feet (61 x 61 x 122cm).
- Ideally, provide an adult male chameleon with a cage with dimensions of 3 x 3 x 4 feet (91 x 91 x 122cm).
- The most suitable cage for veiled chameleons is a mesh vivarium, although a glass terrarium will suffice (especially in cold climates due to heat conservation).
- You will need two types of lamps in your enclosure - for heat and for UVB light.
- UVB exposure is essential for your chameleon - without enough UVB light, he will be more susceptible to nutritional deficiencies and metabolic bone disease.

- You should arrange the heat lamps in your chameleon's cage so that one end is hot and the other end cool.

- The hotter end (for basking) should be at least 95°F/35°C reducing to around 75°F/24°C at the cooler end.

- In the basking area, position at least one lamp 6 to 8 inches (15 to 20cm) above a branch where your chameleon can perch.

- Plan to keep the lights in your chameleon's enclosure lit for 10 to 12 hours per day.

- You need to supply your chameleon's vivarium with plants, branches and vines to give him something to climb on.

- Some of the best veiled chameleon plants to use include hibiscus, ficus and dracaena.

- It is not necessary to use substrate in the vivarium - it may be easier to clean without it.

- You will need to mist the tank for one or two minutes twice a day to keep the humidity up and to provide your chameleon with drinking water.

- The vivarium should be cleaned and sanitized at least once a week, including walls and food bowls.

3) Feeding and Nutritional Needs

- The veiled chameleon is technically omnivorous in the wild but mainly insectivorous in captivity.

- The veiled chameleon diet is varied in order to achieve balanced nutrition and to prevent deficiencies.

- A healthy veiled chameleon diet should provide calcium to phosphorus ratio of 2:1.

- Gut-loading feeder insects is essential, in order to increase their nutritional value.

- If you raise your own insects, gut-load them with a variety of foods including greens, carrots, fruit and fish food.

- Regular calcium supplementation is required to prevent deficiency in veiled chameleons.

- Dust feeder insects several times a week with powdered calcium supplements by adding it to the bag and shaking.

- Potential feeder insects for veiled chameleons include crickets, mealworms, wax worms, grasshoppers, silkworms, hornworms, flies and roaches.

- Some veiled chameleons will eat vegetables, but are not a significant part of their diet - don't worry if yours doesn't.

- Do not feed too many wax worms, mealworms or houseflies - they have low calcium to phosphorus ratio.

- Feeding quota will depend on age - feed juveniles daily as much as they will eat.

- Adult veiled chameleons will generally eat 12 to 24 crickets (or similar insects) every other day.

- Offer insects in a feeder cup, free-roaming or a combination of both.

- Again, make sure you mist the cage for 1 to 2 minutes daily to provide your chameleon with drinking water.

4) Information about Breeding

- Veiled chameleons are oviparous breeders, meaning they lay eggs rather than giving birth to live, fully developed young.
- Females of the species tend to have shorter life expectancy due to the rigor of bearing eggs.
- Males reach sexual maturity around 4-5 months of age, females closer to 6.
- Veiled chameleons should not be bred until they are at least 8 inches (20cm) ideally, 12 inches (30.5cm) long.
- Signs that a female is receptive to breeding include neutral coloration and ignoring or walking away from the male.
- Signs that a female is unreceptive include black coloring, gaping, puffed neck and running away.
- The mating process takes between 10 and 40 minutes from start to completion.
- Once the female is inseminated she will turn black with blue or yellow spots.
- The germination period for females lasts on average between 3 and 5 weeks.
- The average clutch size is between 12 and 20 eggs.

- A nesting box filled with 12 inches (30.5cm) of moist substrate should be provided after the 20th day of gestation.
- To reduce frequency of reproduction, females should be fed every other day and kept at temperatures no higher than 83°F (28°C).
- Eggs should be removed from the nesting box and incubated in a container of moist vermiculate at a temperature between 73° and 80°F (23° to 27°C).
- Veiled chameleon eggs take between 6 and 13 months to develop (8 to 10 on average).
- Hatchlings can be fed pinhead crickets, as many as they will eat dusted with calcium powder.
- Young hatchlings should be separated according to sex after 2 months of age.

Appendix A: Helpful Resources

This book is full of useful information about veiled chameleons and their care, but there is no reason not to further your knowledge about this species. You might for example, have specific questions about where to get a vivarium for your chameleon or you might be wondering what kind of accessories you are likely to find in your area. For this information and more, use the helpful resources in this chapter for the following:

- General Information
- Vivariums
- Feeding
- Naming

1) General Information for Veiled Chameleons

United States Websites:

"Veiled Chameleons." www.peteducation.com

"The Veiled Chameleon (Chamaeleo calyptratus) Purchase and Captive Care." www.kingsnake.com

"Veiled Chameleon." Smithsonian National Zoological Park - Reptiles and Amphibians. www.nationalzoo.si.edu

United Kingdom Websites:

"Veiled Chameleon." www.thejunglezoo.co.uk

"Veiled Chameleon Care Sheet." UK Chameleons. www.martinsreptiles.co.uk

"Yemen Chameleon." www.exotic-pets.co.uk

"Veiled Chameleon Care Sheet." www.thereptilian.co.uk

Visit our website www.VeiledChameleonsCare.com if you are interested in becoming an affiliate for this book.

2) Veiled Chameleon Vivariums

United States Websites:

"Aluminum Screen Cage Ultimate Chameleon Package."
www.lllreptile.com

"Reptile Habitats." Doctors Foster and Smith.
www.drsfostersmith.com

"Veiled Chameleon." www.zoomed.com

United Kingdom Websites:

"Housing." www.chameleonden.co.uk

"Screen Enclosures." www.chameleonworldmuji.co.uk

"Enclosures/Habitat."
www.raisingkittytheveiledchameleon.blogspot.co.uk

"Reptile Terrariums and Vivariums." www.seapets.co.uk

3) Feeding Veiled Chameleons

United States Websites:

"Chameleon Feeding – What a Chameleon Eats."
www.reptileknowledge.com

"Feeding Baby Chameleons." www.chameleonparadise.net

"Feeding." Kammerflage Kreations.
www.chameleonsonly.com

United Kingdom Websites:

"Feeding and Supplementation."
www.chameleonden.co.uk

"Yemen Chameleon." www.captivebred.co.uk

"Feeding Chameleons."
www.webgazette.co.uk/wordpress-
themes/chameleon/feeding-chameleons

"Yemen Chameleon." www.evolutionreptiles.co.uk

4) Naming Your Veiled Chameleon

United States Websites:

"4 Rules for Naming a Pet."
www.parenting.com/article/4-rules-for-naming-a-pet

"It's All in the Name." www.newpet.com

"Pet Naming Tips." www.bowwow.com.au

United Kingdom Websites:

"Cool Names for Cats, Dogs and Other Pets."
www.nameyourpet.co.uk

"Pet Names." www.pet-names.org.uk

"Pet Name Calculator." www.lovingyourpet.co.uk/pet-names/calculator/

5) Other Useful Websites

"HouseCarers" Pet sitting - great for finding people to look after your veiled chameleon (and home) while you are away.

www.housecarers.com

"Crickets and Mealworm Breeding."

www.cricketsbreedingmadesimple.com

"Advanced Insect Breeding Systems."

www.zegaenterprises.com.au

Visit our website www.VeiledChameleonsCare.com for our contact details or if you are interested in becoming an affiliate for this book.

Appendix B: Raising Insects at Home

Because veiled chameleons follow an insectivorous diet, you will need to have a variety of live insects on hand at all times. Even though you can find certain types of insects at your local pet store, or order them online, it may be more economical to raise them yourself at home. In this section you will receive tips for raising some of the most common feeder insects at home.

1) Crickets

Items Required:
- 15 to 20 large live crickets.
- 10 gallon (38 liter) aquarium.
- 40 watt bulb in a dome reflector.
- Coconut substrate.
- Commercial cricket diet.
- Cardboard tubes, egg crates, etc.

Crickets can be kept in a 10 gallon (38 liter) aquarium lined with coconut substrate. Ideally, the aquarium should be kept at a temperature between 75° and 85°F (24° to 29°C). All you should need in order to maintain this temperature, as long as the crickets are kept indoors, is a 40 watt bulb in a dome reflector. The reflector will help to direct the light and the heat it produces into the aquarium. Provide the aquarium with egg crates, toilet paper tubes, and other objects on which the crickets can climb and in which they can hide.

To care for your crickets, mist the aquarium every other day with water to keep the substrate moist. You should also supply a damp sponge in a shallow dish as a water source – keep the sponge wet, but do not fill the dish with water or your crickets could drown. Feed your crickets a commercial cricket diet supplemented with fresh fruits and vegetables such as lettuce, kale, apples and orange slices. These foods will help to hydrate your crickets as well as keep them nourished.

2) Mealworms

Items Required:
- 2 dozen live mealworms
- 10 gallon (38 liter) aquarium
- Oats or bran
- Potatoes

Mealworms can be kept in any lidded container of appropriate size, but a 10 gallon (38 liter) aquarium is the easiest option – just ensure it has a lid. Fill the container about half full with oats, bran or a combined mixture of both - this will serve as bedding for the mealworms to dig in but also as a source of food. In a shallow dish place half of a potato which will provide moisture for the mealworms as well as another food source, this will need to be replaced every few days. Add the mealworms to the container and wait for them to breed.

The mealworms will first pupate then after about 2 weeks will turn into beetles and lay eggs. The eggs will be too small for you to see but, when they hatch, the larvae (mealworms) will start to grow and repeat the cycle. If at any point you find you have too many mealworms, you can start to store them in lidded plastic containers with a little substrate in the refrigerator. This will stop their development and make them available as food for your veiled chameleon.

3) Cockroaches

Items Required:
- 10 gallon (38 liter) aquarium.
- Insect substrate.
- Fresh fruit and vegetables .
- Egg crates, branches etc.

The key to raising cockroaches as feeder insects is ideally to select a non-climbing species, but be sure to keep a lid on the tank to prevent them from escaping and infesting your home. Smearing Vaseline along the upper two inches of the glass inside the tank will also help to deter the roaches from climbing out. Keep in mind that a 10 gallon (38 liter) aquarium can house hundreds of small roaches, but only approx 30 of the larger species such as Madagascar hissing cockroaches. If you plan to raise this species, consider using a larger aquarium or several small ones.

Line the bottom of the aquarium with insect-friendly substrate such as coconut fiber and equip the tank with egg crates, branches and other objects on which the roaches can climb. Keep the temperature fairly warm, around 80°F/27°C as some species will not breed below this temperature. Feed your roaches a variety of fruits and vegetables as well as some dried pet food to meet their need for protein. To provide your roaches with water, water crystals are the best option. As long as you maintain the correct conditions, the roaches should breed readily leaving you with an endless supply of food for your veiled chameleon.

4) Buying Insects Online

If you prefer not to raise your feeder insects at home, or if you need some insects to start your colony, the cheapest option is to buy them in bulk online. Below you will find a collection of resources for buying feeder insects online:

Feeder Insects in the U.S.:

Backwater Reptiles; www.backwaterreptiles.com

LLLReptile; www.lllreptile.com

Big Apple Pet Supply; www.bigappleherp.com/reptile-supplies

Armstrong Crickets; www.armstrongcrickets.com

Feeder Insects in the U.K.:

FaunaTech; www.faunatech.co.uk

Livefood UK; www.livefoods.co.uk

HML Livefoods; www.hml-livefood-deliveries.co.uk

Appendix C: Glossary of Useful Terms

Ambient Temperature – the overall temperature in your veiled chameleon's enclosure.

Arboreal – refers to an animal that lives primarily in the trees (opposite being terrestrial).

Casque – a helmet-like structure on top of the chameleon's head also referred to as a crest.

Ectothermic- an animal that relies on the temperature of it's environment to regulate it's body heat.

Gravid – an egg bearing female.

Gut-Loading – the process of feeding insects healthy foods so the nutrients are transferred to your chameleon when he eats them.

Hatchling – the name given to a baby veiled chameleon or baby Yemen chameleon after it hatches.

Humidity – the amount of water vapor in the air.

Insectivore – a species that derives the majority of its nutrition from eating insects.

Oviparous – a type of animal that lays eggs.

Prehensile Tail – a tale capable of wrapping and grasping; acting as a fifth appendage.

Sexual Dimorphism – marked physical differences, between the sexes of one species.

Tarsal Spur – a spur found on the back of the heel in male veiled chameleons, used during breeding.

Vivarium – an enclosure used for keeping pets.

Zygodactyly – refers to the arrangement of toes in birds and chameleons; first and last digits facing backward, the middle two facing forward.

Index

D

E

F

G

H

I

J

K

L

M

U

V

W

Y

Notes

CPSIA information can be obtained
at www.ICGtesting.com
Printed in the USA
BVHW041319251120
593999BV00008B/650

9 781910 517024